NAMES DON'T HAVE AN AGE

By Steph Coffield

Copyright © 2024 Steph Coffield

All rights reserved. No part of this publication may be reproduced, stored in retrieval system, or transmitted in any form or by any means, electronic, mechanical, photocopying, recording, or otherwise, without written permission by the author.

ISBNs
Paperback: 979-8-218-42713-9
eBook: 979-8-218-42714-6

First edition, July 2024

This is a work of fiction. Names, characters, places, and individuals either are the product of the author's imagination or are used fictitiously, and any resemblance to actual persons, living or dead, businesses, companies, events, or locales is entirely coincidental.

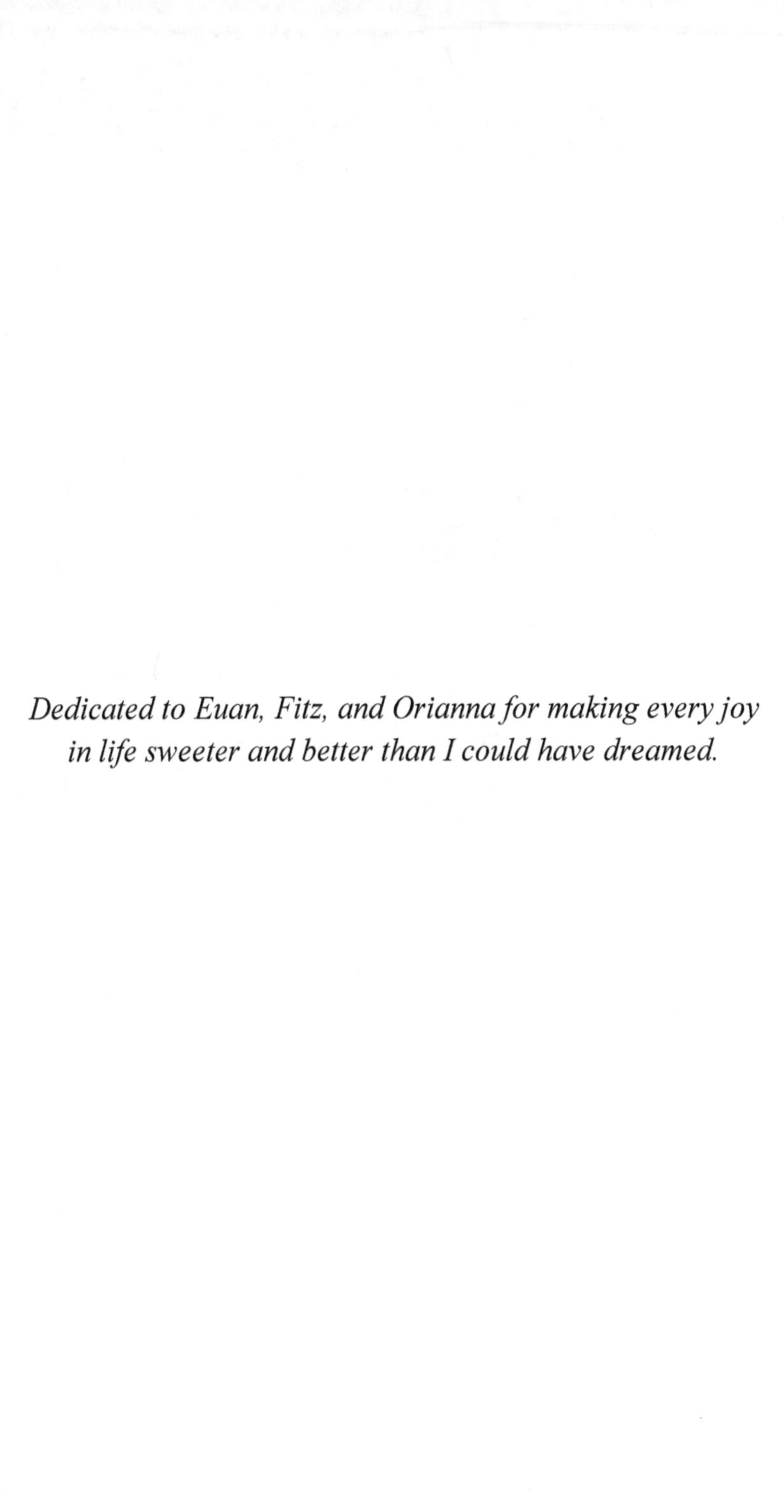

Dedicated to Euan, Fitz, and Orianna for making every joy in life sweeter and better than I could have dreamed.

TABLE OF CONTENTS

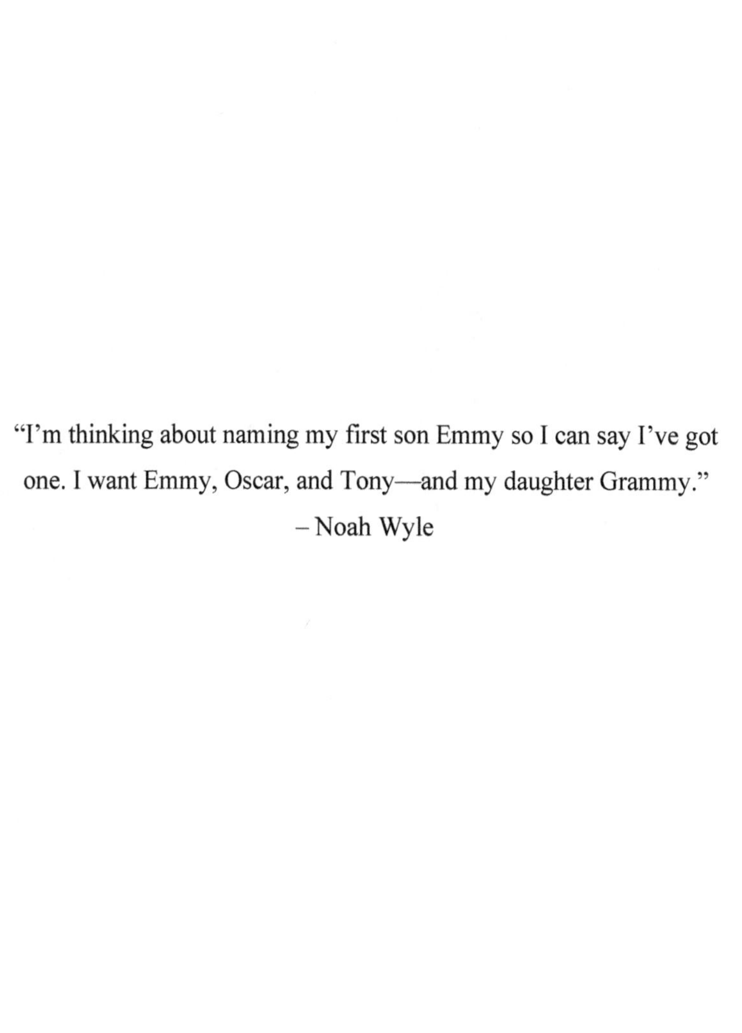

"I'm thinking about naming my first son Emmy so I can say I've got one. I want Emmy, Oscar, and Tony—and my daughter Grammy."

– Noah Wyle

INTRODUCTION

IMAGINE FOR A MOMENT you are witnessing a beautiful sunset for the very first time. The colors you observe are like nothing you've ever seen before. Then, someone hands you a piece of paper with a list of colors and tells you to select the ones you see in the sunset. You might choose to call the orangey color *magenta*, the yellow hue *chartreuse*, and the purple color *crimson*. But someone else might see the orange as more of a *tawny brown*, and they might label the reddish tones *hot pink* and completely disregard any yellow or purple.

Regardless of how we label the colors of a sunset, they do not change the splendor of the mingling colors. We can name them orange, yellow, and red—or rust, gold, and burgundy—and their picturesque tranquility remains unchanged. This concept of labels and their relationship to essence extends to a person's name. It holds nothing on its own. It is merely a label and an empty vessel until it is attached to an actual human being. Generalizations and regional trends aside (because they *can* offer minimal data), on a greater scale, names do not give you insight into a person's economic status, location, race, gender, or age.

Welcome to a space where we avoid making assumptions about others and where *Names Don't Have an Age*. Previously, we discussed how *Names Don't Have a Gender* and that is truer than ever! The conversation about feminine and masculine names and the use of them has become much more fluid and that makes my heart very happy.

This book is a compilation of my favorite names from a myriad of themes, genres, and decades. Each one of them has been handpicked to live on these pages as inspiration for you.

Many of these themes are subjective. What makes one name sporty and what makes another old money-inspired? It's based on lived experiences and real people, of course. I've also labeled groups of names by adjectives like "playful" or "quirky," where I chose a name based on consonant sounds and uncommon letters. Perhaps the missing piece is *there is always room for change*. We can change the quality and characteristics of any name with a different perspective.

Some themes leave less to interpretation. For example, I've categorized names by syllable count, origin, rarity, and time period.

Have you ever expressed how much someone embodies their name? As in, "Oh, she is a total Paula!" Or, "He acts just like a Kevin." But what if Kevin was an Alexander? I bet you'd be saying the same thing. This is why we cannot claim certain names are "too old" for babies. I promise you every single Ethel and Oscar were once newborns as well.

My favorite example to demonstrate *Names Don't Have an Age* is Dolly Parton. Her given name is Dolly Rebecca Parton and she was born in 1946. No one bats an eye at Dolly's whimsical, childlike, and nickname-inspired name, do they? She is a powerful musician, singer, songwriter, philanthropist, and more, and her name has nothing to do with the amazing life she created for herself. At present, we might associate the name Dolly with country music, a sweet Southern personality, and big, blonde hair—but that is temporary. The next famous Dolly could be different in every way.

Let's look at my name: Stephanie. It is a quintessential '80s name. I was born in 1983, so while it fits, it doesn't mean every Stephanie was born in the 1980s. Every so often I get a comment online from people asking how a name consultant has such a boring name… *don't they realize I didn't name myself?*

And, actually, I love my name. My mom is a teacher and she had the sweetest little girl called Stephanie in her class at the time. My dad agreed it was a great name and that was that. My middle name is Lynn, a name that comes from my mom as well. Her name is Vicky Lynn, a combination chosen by my maternal grandma's grandmother. I knew that if I had a daughter, I would carry on the tradition and now I have an Orianna Lynn.

Don't worry about my dad, they gave my sister the feminine version of his name, Gene, and her name is Melissa Jean. My brother and youngest sibling was given my mom's maiden name in the middle spot back before it was trendy. His name is Joshua Durow. I love our theme of names with three syllables; Mom said it was intentional. And now, I've given both of my boys my maiden name for their middle name: my sons are Euan Limesand and Fitz Limesand.

While I don't regret it, if I were getting married today, I'm not sure I would have changed my last name to my husband's. It's been neat to watch the archaic trend become decreasingly popular and while I've only dabbled in helping couples choose a new family name, I'm excited to help more in the future. I'm a big fan of combining parts of the two surnames or as social media has suggested, picking the "cooler sounding" last name and using it for the entire family. Not a bad idea at all.

I digress; let's get down to business. If you are trying to name a baby and you are feeling pressure or the weight of that decision, know you are not alone. Giving someone a name is a huge decision that will potentially last a lifetime and you're not wrong to take it seriously. But don't forget to have fun as well! Browsing for names is (obviously) one of my favorite pastimes and I'm so glad I get to do it all the time.

One of the greatest ways to connect with someone is over their name. I hope you feel more connected to me knowing my name. It's the very first thing we ask when we meet someone new, "What's your name?" I'll tell you a secret: I go by Steph in my business because my social media handles are all Names With Steph and consequently, that's what everyone calls me—but, if I'm being perfectly honest, I used to hate the nickname Steph. It's way too short and harsh for me; I find Stephanie to be so elegant and beautiful sounding.

The thing is, the more I learn about names, the more I adore them and the harder it is to find ones I truly dislike. The same goes for Steph. I'm proud to be Steph now. It's actually a pretty cute name. It's a good lesson in how we should all be open to changing our minds when presented with new information.

I have been sharing baby name inspiration on the internet for more than three years now and reading personal messages of people's unique names never gets old. My favorite is when someone tells me I have helped them to like—or even love—their own name after struggling to do so for years. Because the truth is, we cannot guarantee our children will resonate with their name the way we do as their parents.

"Your name is a gift you can return if it doesn't fit."
-ANDREA GIBSON, POET

I find this sentiment both powerful and loving. As a parent you are saying: *I give you this name but if one day in the future you find it doesn't feel right anymore, you can change it. I love you more than I love your name.*

Important Insights:

While the majority of my work is with soon-to-be parents, I have also done name orders for authors' character names, business names, pet names, and more. This book is for everyone. You can be naming a child, an animal, a plant, or a vehicle, but I promise you'll find something you love in these pages.

Each name was hand-selected by me and meticulously placed in its category. My goal is always for zero repeat names in each book (but that doesn't mean you won't see both Olivia and Oliver, because let's be real, that would be tough).

You don't need a name book with 100,000+ names in it, that read like dictionaries and are full of the same names over *and over* again. Plus, it's easy to get overwhelmed with so many choices.

I pick names that resonate with me and I can picture being used. I categorize them by popular and uncommon because I have found that to be one of the biggest deciding factors for my own clients.

I do my best to share information as accurately as possible, but many names have multiple origins, meanings, and pronunciations. Further, while I am providing inspiration and insight, it is your job to research the name you choose for your child.

This book is intentionally genderless (and ageless!) so you can make your choice based on what works for your family. My advice is to keep your favorite names to yourself because as the adage goes, "Opinions are like assholes, everybody has one and they usually stink."

'50s FUN

Popular

	Name	Origin	Meaning
☐	**David**	Hebrew	beloved
☐	**Debra**	Hebrew	bee
☐	**John**	Hebrew	God is gracious
☐	**Linda**	Spanish, Portuguese, Germanic	soft, tender, beautiful
☐	**Mark**	Latin	to be warlike
☐	**Mary**	English from Hebrew, Egyptian	bitter, beloved, wished-for child, rebelliousness
☐	**Nancy**	English from Hebrew	grace, favored
☐	**Paul**	Latin	small
☐	**Sandra**	Italian from Greek	protector of humanity
☐	**Thomas**	Aramaic	twin

<u>Uncommon</u>

☐	**Alvis**	Old Norse	noble friend, elf friend or all wise
☐	**Dewitt**	Flemish	blond
☐	**Eldridge**	English	sage, wise ruler
☐	**Fritz**	German	peaceful ruler
☐	**Lex**	Greek, from Alexander	protector of humanity
☐	**Madonna**	Latin	my lady
☐	**Rubin**	Hebrew	behold, a son
☐	**Talmadge** TOW-mihj	English from Old French	pouch wallet or mask
☐	**Velda**	German	power, rule
☐	**Zelma**	German	God's helmet

'60s VIBES

Popular

☐	**Brenda**	Old Norse, Celtic	sword, a flame
☐	**Bruce**	Scottish from Norman	the willowlands
☐	**Christine**	French from Greek	Christian
☐	**Julie**	Latin, Greek	youthful, downy-bearded, sky father
☐	**Lisa**	English, Hebrew, and more	God is my oath
☐	**Patricia**	Latin	noble, patrician
☐	**Richard**	Old German	brave ruler
☐	**Ronald**	Old Norse	advice, counsel, ruler
☐	**Steven**	English from Greek	garland, crown
☐	**Vicky**	Latin	victory

Uncommon

	Name	Origin	Meaning
☐	**Barbie**	Latin	foreign, stranger
☐	**Boris**	Slavic	small, battle glory
☐	**Bud**	English, American	friend
☐	**Cordell**	Old French, English	maker or seller of rope or cord
☐	**Gilda**	English, Celtic, German	covered with gold
☐	**Hershel**	Yiddish	deer
☐	**Major**	Latin	greater, a military rank
☐	**Millicent**	German	strong in work
☐	**Nestor**	Greek	traveler
☐	**Wilford**	Old English	willow ford

'70s STYLE

Popular

☐	**Brian**	Irish	high, noble
☐	**Jeffrey**	German, English	pledge of peace
☐	**Jennifer**	Cornish from Welsh	white phantom, white shadow, white wave
☐	**Kimberly**	English	Cyneburga's field
☐	**Michael**	Hebrew	who is like God?
☐	**Michelle**	French from Hebrew	who is like God?
☐	**Scott**	English	from Scotland, painted warrior
☐	**Tiffany**	English from Greek	manifestation of God
☐	**Tracy**	French	of Thracius
☐	**Timothy**	Greek	honoring God

<u>Uncommon</u>

☐	**Doyle**	Irish	dark stranger
☐	**Judd**	Hebrew from Jordan	to flow down
☐	**Kermit**	English from Irish	meaning unknown
☐	**Lorne**	Latin, or Scottish place name	laurel
☐	**Lydell**	English, Scottish	of the Liddel
☐	**Marnie**	English from Latin	of the sea
☐	**Mitzi**	German	bitter or star of the sea
☐	**Torrence**	Gaelic	from the craggy hills
☐	**Tressa**	Cornish	third
☐	**Vonda**	German	wanderer

'80s FLAIR

Popular

☐ **Daniel** — Hebrew — God is my judge

☐ **Heather** — English — evergreen flowering plant

☐ **Joshua*** — Hebrew — God is salvation

☐ **Justin** — Latin — just, righteous

☐ **Matthew** — Hebrew — gift of God

☐ **Melissa*** — Greek — honeybee

☐ **Nicole** — French from Greek — people of victory

☐ **Robert** — English from German — bright fame

☐ **Ryan** — Irish — little king

☐ **Stephanie*** — Greek — garland, crown

*I put my siblings' names as well as my own in this decade because we were all born in the '80s and each of our names are in the top ten list for this decade.

<u>Uncommon</u>

	Name	Origin	Meaning
☐	**Dewey**	English from Welsh	beloved
☐	**Elvin**	English, variation of Alvin	noble friend, elf friend
☐	**Hilda**	German, Norse	battle
☐	**Keely**	Irish	slender
☐	**Kip**	Greek, Latin	bearer of Christ
☐	**Marcelino** mar-seh-LEE-no	Spanish, Portuguese	unknown
☐	**Mona**	Irish, English	noble one, my lady, and more
☐	**Shavonne**	English from Irish (phonetic spelling of Siobhan)	God is gracious
☐	**Samson**	Hebrew	sun
☐	**Tana**	Russian, Greek, Slavic, Spanish	fairy queen, thought, sweetheart

'90s INSPIRED

Popular

- ☐ **Ashley** — Old English — ash tree clearing
- ☐ **Brandon** — English — broom covered hill
- ☐ **Brittany** — English from French — from Bretagne
- ☐ **Caitlin** — Irish from Greek — pure
- ☐ **Christopher** — Greek, Latin — bearer of Christ
- ☐ **Jessica** — English from Hebrew, from Iscah — to behold
- ☐ **Joseph** — Hebrew — he will add
- ☐ **Samantha** — Hebrew — told by God
- ☐ **Sarah** — Hebrew — princess, lady, noblewoman
- ☐ **Trevor** — Welsh — large village

<u>Uncommon</u>

☐	**Darcy**	English from French	from Arcy or dark one
☐	**Hernán** h-ER-nuhn	Spanish	gentle traveler
☐	**Jodie**	Hebrew	Jehovah increases
☐	**Kia**	African, Scandinavian, and more	not enough sources
☐	**Marjorie**	English from Margaret	pearl
☐	**Morris**	English	dark-skinned
☐	**Rusty**	English from French	redhead
☐	**Sally**	Hebrew from Sarah	princess, noblewoman
☐	**Sherry**	French, variation on Cheri	beloved
☐	**Wendell**	German, Dutch	wanderer, a Vandal

Y2K

Popular

☐	**Abigail**	Hebrew	my father is joyful
☐	**Hannah**	Hebrew	grace
☐	**Jacob**	Hebrew	holder of the heel or supplanter
☐	**Jonathan**	Hebrew	gift of Jehovah
☐	**Kayla**	Hebrew	laurel, crown
☐	**Lauren**	English from Latin	from Laurentum or bay laurel
☐	**Madison**	English	son of Maud
☐	**Morgan**	Welsh	sea-born, sea-song, sea-circle
☐	**Tyler**	English	maker of tiles
☐	**Zachary**	Hebrew	the Lord has remembered

<u>Uncommon</u>

☐	**Bonnie**	Scottish	pretty, beautiful, cheerful
☐	**Brennon**	Irish	rain, moisture, drop, or sorrow
☐	**Gia**	Italian	God is gracious
☐	**Harvey**	French	battle worthy
☐	**Kennedy**	Irish	helmeted head
☐	**Korbin**	Latin	crow, raven
☐	**Lourdes** LOORD or LOORDZ	Basque	craggy slope
☐	**Shea** SHAY	Irish	admirable, stately
☐	**Yasmeen**	Arabic, Persian	jasmine flower
☐	**Zander**	Greek	defending men

ONE SYLLABLE

Popular

☐	**Blake**	English	dark or pale
☐	**Dean**	English	church official
☐	**Eve**	Hebrew	life
☐	**Faye**	English	fairy or faith
☐	**Grant**	Scottish	great, large
☐	**Jude**	Hebrew	praised
☐	**Rae**	Hebrew, variation of Ray	ewe
☐	**Sean**	Irish	God is gracious
☐	**Tripp**	American	third
☐	**Zane**	Hebrew, possible variation of John	God is gracious

<u>Uncommon</u>

☐	**Bee**	Latin	she who brings happiness, or insect name
☐	**Charm**	Middle English	to attract or lucky token
☐	**Cy** SIE	Persian	sun
☐	**Gene**	Greek	wellborn
☐	**Lance**	Old German	land
☐	**Penn**	English	enclosure, hill
☐	**Rue**	English	regret
☐	**Tam**	Scottish	twin
☐	**Vern**	English	alder grove
☐	**Wynn** WIN	English, Welsh	friend, white, fair, blessed

TWO SYLLABLES

<u>Popular</u>

☐ **Adam**	Hebrew	man (son) of the red earth
☐ **Clara**	Latin	bright, clear
☐ **Courtney**	English from French	place name or short nose
☐ **Finley**	Scottish, Irish	fair-haired hero, courageous
☐ **Isaac**	Hebrew	to laugh, to rejoice
☐ **Lucy**	English from Latin	light
☐ **Maxwell**	Scottish	great stream
☐ **Parker**	Old English	park keeper
☐ **Sophie**	French from Greek	wisdom
☐ **Tatum**	English	Tata's homestead

<u>Uncommon</u>

☐ **Amos**
AY-mus
Hebrew — to carry, carried by God

☐ **Colby**
Old Norse, English — from a coal town

☐ **Edith**
English — prosperous in war

☐ **Harley**
English — hare's meadow

☐ **Maren**
Latin — sea

☐ **Opal**
Sanskrit — jewel

☐ **Otis**
German — wealthy

☐ **Selby**
English — from the willow farm

☐ **Vera**
Russian from Latin — faith, truth

☐ **Watson**
English — son of Walter

THREE SYLLABLES

<u>Popular</u>

☐ **Atticus**   Latin   from Attica

☐ **Benjamin**   Hebrew   son of the right hand

☐ **Eleanor**   Old French   unknown possibly light

☐ **Gianna**   Italian   God is gracious

☐ **Harrison**   English   son of Harry

☐ **Lorenzo**   Italian, Spanish   from Laurentum, laurel crown

☐ **Miranda**   Latin   admirable, wonderful

☐ **Nicholas**   Greek   victory of the people

☐ **Rosalie**   French from Latin   rose

☐ **Sullivan**   Irish   dark-eyed one

<u>Uncommon</u>

☐ **Anniston**	English	town of Anis or Agnes town
☐ **Augustine**	Latin	exalted, venerable, great
☐ **Elodie** EH-luh-dee	French	foreign riches
☐ **Finnian**	Irish	fair one
☐ **Indigo**	English from Greek	dark blue dye, Indian dye
☐ **Paloma**	Spanish	dove
☐ **Priscilla**	Latin	ancient, venerable
☐ **Sybella** si-BELL-aa	Greek	prophetess, seer, oracle
☐ **Tennyson**	English	son of Dennis
☐ **Viveca** VIV-uh-kah	Scandinavian	alive, war fortress

FOUR SYLLABLES

Popular

- ☐ **Antonio** — Italian, Spanish — unknown

- ☐ **Emmanuel** — Hebrew — God is with us

- ☐ **Ezekiel**
  uh-ZEE-kee-uhl — Hebrew — God will strengthen

- ☐ **Gabriella** — Italian, Spanish from Hebrew — God is my strength

- ☐ **Giovanoli**
  jo-van-OH-lee — Italian — God is gracious

- ☐ **Jeremiah** — Hebrew — God will raise, to exalt

- ☐ **Liliana** — Italian, Spanish — lily

- ☐ **Olivia** — Latin — olive tree

- ☐ **Penelope** — Greek — type of bird or weaver

- ☐ **Veronica** — Latin — bringing victory, true image

<u>Uncommon</u>

☐ **Andromeda**	Greek	to be mindful of mankind
☐ **Aurelian** aw-RAY-lee-uhn	Latin	golden
☐ **Caterina**	Italian, Catalan	pure
☐ **Esperanza**	Spanish	hope, expectation
☐ **Henrietta**	French, German, and more	home ruler
☐ **Horatio** hr-AY-shee-ow	English from Latin	hour, time, season
☐ **Mahalia** ma-HAH-lee-ah	Hebrew	tenderness
☐ **Octavian**	Latin	eighth
☐ **Oleander**	Greek	Mediterranean shrub
☐ **Xiomara** see-OH-ma-ra	Spanish	ready for battle

FEWER THAN 10 BABIES (2023)

Girl's List

☐	**Avella (6)**	Spanish	place name, hazelnut
☐	**Blanche (8)**	French	white
☐	**Devereaux (6)** DEV-eh-roe	French	banks of the river
☐	**Evoleth (9)**	English	invented name
☐	**Islarose (6)**	combination of Scottish or Spanish and Latin	island + rose
☐	**Kerrington (6)**	English from French Carrington	rocky settlement
☐	**Kindred (9)**	English	family
☐	**Storri (7)**	English, variation of Story	tale
☐	**Vintage (5)**	English from Latin	to take away a gathering of grapes
☐	**Wrinley (7)**	English, combination of Brinley + Wrenley	invented name

Boy's List

- ☐ **Calhoun (8)**
  kal-HOON — Scottish — from the narrow woods

- ☐ **Crash (8)** — English — to collide violently

- ☐ **Delroy (9)** — Old French — of the king

- ☐ **Hickory (7)** — English — tree name

- ☐ **Kipling (6)** — English — Cyppel's people

- ☐ **Murdock (8)** — Irish, Scottish — sea warrior

- ☐ **Renton (7)** — English — possibly settlement of the roe deer

- ☐ **Roark (9)** — Old Irish — hero, champion

- ☐ **Tylus (7)** — English, combination of Tyler + Titus — maker of tiles, title of honor

- ☐ **Zee (8)** — multicultural — varied

ANTIQUES

Popular

☐	**Alice**	German	noble
☐	**Arthur**	Celtic	bear
☐	**Dorothy**	English from Greek	gift of God
☐	**Edward**	English	wealthy guardian
☐	**Felix**	Latin	happy, fortunate, lucky
☐	**Hazel**	Old English	the hazelnut tree
☐	**Lydia**	Greek	from Lydia
☐	**Oscar**	Old English, Irish	dear friend, God spear
☐	**Theodore**	English from Greek	gift of God
☐	**Violet**	English from Latin	purple, purple flower

<u>Uncommon</u>

☐	**Adelia**	Germanic	noble, nobility
☐	**Booker**	English	scribe, book binder
☐	**Effie**	English from Greek	well-spoken, pleasant speech
☐	**Enoch** ee-NOK	Hebrew	dedicated, disciplined
☐	**Loveday**	Old English	beloved day
☐	**Permelia**	English	all honey/sweetness
☐	**Ransom**	English	warrior's shield
☐	**Sumner**	English	summoner
☐	**Vernon**	English	place of alders, springlike
☐	**Zola**	African	piece of earth or calm, peaceful

ARTISTS

Popular

☐	**Amy**	French, Latin	beloved
☐	**Andy**	Greek	strong, manly
☐	**Georgia**	English from Greek	farmer
☐	**Jackson**	English	son of Jack (John)
☐	**Leonardo**	Italian, Spanish from German	brave lion
☐	**Louise**	French, English, Dutch	famous warrior
☐	**Pablo**	Spanish	small
☐	**Peter**	Greek	rock or stone
☐	**Raphael**	Hebrew	God has healed
☐	**Vincent**	Latin	conquering

This list includes references to the artists Amy Sherald, Andy Warhol, Georgia O'Keeffe, Jackson Pollock, Leonardo da Vinci, Louise Bourgeois, Pablo Picasso, Peter Paul Rubens, Raffaello Sanzio, and Vincent van Gogh.

<u>Uncommon</u>

☐	**Artemisia** aar-tuh-MEE-zhuh	Greek	unknown, possibly safe or a butcher
☐	**Bernice**	Greek	bringer of victory
☐	**Claude**	French from Latin	lame
☐	**Donatello**	Italian, Spanish	a gift
☐	**Edmonia**	English	rich guardian
☐	**Frida**	German	peace
☐	**Kara**	Italian, Irish, or Norse	beloved, dear, wild stormy one
☐	**Leonora**	Italian	unknown possibly light
☐	**Rembrandt**	Dutch	advice or counsel, fire or sword
☐	**Tanner**	English	leather tanner

This list includes references to the artists Artemisia Gentileschi, Bernice Bing, Claude Monet, Donatello, Edmonia Lewis, Frida Kahlo, Kara Walker, Leonora Carrington, Rembrandt van Rijn, and Henry Ossawa Tanner.

BEACHY

<u>Popular</u>

	Name	Origin	Meaning
☐	**Coast**	English	land near the sea
☐	**Dylan**	Welsh	son of the sea, born of the ocean
☐	**Isla** EYE-la	Scottish, Spanish	island
☐	**Kai**	Hawaiian	sea
☐	**Marina**	Latin	from the sea
☐	**Marlow**	English	driftwood
☐	**Pearl**	English from Latin	pearl, precious gemstone
☐	**Ross**	Scottish, English	headland, peninsula
☐	**Sandy**	Greek	defending people
☐	**Sunny**	English	cheerful, sunshine

<u>Uncommon</u>

☐	**Caspian**	Latin	white
☐	**Cove**	English	small bay or small coastal inlet
☐	**Delmar**	Spanish	of the sea
☐	**Havilah** HAV-i-la	Hebrew	varied, stretch of sand
☐	**Ibiza** ee-BEE-zuh	Arabic	land
☐	**Mervyn**	Welsh	sea hill
☐	**Oceana**	Greek	ocean
☐	**Thalassa** thaa-LAA-suh	Greek	sea
☐	**Ula**	Celtic	gem of the sea
☐	**Zale**	Greek	sea-strength

BEAUTIFUL SOUNDING

Popular

☐	**Alexander**	Greek	defending men
☐	**Evander**	Greek, Scottish	good man, bow warrior
☐	**Francesca**	Italian	from France or free one
☐	**Isabel**	Spanish	pledged to God
☐	**Julian**	Latin, Greek	youthful, downy-bearded
☐	**Lillian**	English from Latin	lily, pledged to God
☐	**Ophelia**	Greek	help, aid
☐	**Santiago**	Spanish, Portuguese	Saint James
☐	**Vivian**	Latin	life
☐	**Willow**	Old English	willow tree

<u>Uncommon</u>

☐ **Ambrose** Latin immortal

☐ **Beauregard** French beautiful gaze or
BOW-ruh-gaard outlook

☐ **Cordelia** Latin, Celtic heart, daughter of
the sea

☐ **Ellington** English from Ellis' town

☐ **Evangeline** Greek bearer of good news

☐ **Florian** Latin flowering

☐ **Leland** Old English fallow or meadow
land

☐ **Leopold** German brave people

☐ **Marcella** Latin warlike
mar-CHEH-la
or mar-SEH-la

☐ **Philomena** Greek lover of strength,
loved one

BRANDS

Popular

☐	**Bentley**	Old English	meadow or clearing with coarse/bent grass
☐	**Brooks**	English	lives near a brook
☐	**Calvin**	Latin	bald, hairless
☐	**Ford**	English	lives near the ford
☐	**Kate**	English from Greek	pure
☐	**Levi**	Hebrew	joined, united
☐	**Macy**	English from French	from the town of Massy
☐	**Mercedes**	Spanish	mercies, wages, reward
☐	**Stanley**	Old English	stone clearing
☐	**Wilson**	English	son of William

<u>Uncommon</u>

☐	**Allegra**	Italian	cheerful, lively
☐	**Chanel**	French	dweller near the channel or jug, bottle
☐	**Dior**	French	possibly golden
☐	**Dove**	English	dove, a bird
☐	**Evian**	English variation of Evan	God is gracious
☐	**Maybelline**	English, from Mabel	lovable
☐	**Nike**	Greek	victory
☐	**Porsche** POR-shuh	German surname	unknown
☐	**Sephora**	Greek from Hebrew	bird
☐	**Wrangler**	English from German	to dispute, to wrestle

BRITISH MONARCHY

Popular

☐	**Anne**	Hebrew, French, English	grace
☐	**Archie**	German, English	bold, brave
☐	**Camilla**	Italian from Latin	possibly a young religious attendant
☐	**Catherine**	Greek	pure
☐	**Charlotte**	French from German	free person
☐	**Elizabeth**	Hebrew	God is my oath
☐	**George**	Greek	farmer
☐	**Henry**	French, German	estate ruler
☐	**Louis**	French, German	famous warrior
☐	**William**	German	will, helmet or protection

Uncommon

☐ **Albert**	German	noble, bright, famous
☐ **Beatrice**	Latin	she who brings happiness
☐ **Birgitte**	Norse from Gaelic	exalted one
☐ **Diana**	Latin, Greek	divine
☐ **Ernest**	English from German	serious, resolute
☐ **Eugenie**	French from Greek	wellborn, noble
☐ **Lilibet**	Hebrew	God is my oath
☐ **Meghan**	Welsh	pearl
☐ **Philip**	Greek	lover of horses
☐ **Zara**	Arabic, Persian, Hebrew	princess, radiant, shining, blossom

BROADWAY

Popular

- ☐ **Aaron** Hebrew — high mountain, exalted

- ☐ **Audrey** Old English — noble strength

- ☐ **Danny** Hebrew — God is my judge

- ☐ **Evan** Welsh version of John — God is gracious

- ☐ **Jenna** English, from Jennifer — white phantom, white wave

- ☐ **Jeremy** English from Hebrew — God will raise, to exalt

- ☐ **Maria** Latin from Hebrew or Egyptian — bitter, beloved, wished for child, rebelliousness

- ☐ **Molly** English from Hebrew or Egyptian — bitter, beloved, wished for child, rebelliousness

- ☐ **Nathan** Hebrew — he gave, given

- ☐ **Todd** English — fox

This list includes references from shows *Hamilton*, *Little Shop of Horrors*, *Grease*, *Dear Evan Hansen*, *Waitress*, *Be More Chill*, *West Side Story*, *Annie*, *Guys and Dolls*, and *Sweeney Todd*.

<u>Uncommon</u>

☐ **Cosette** French or Greek   little thing or people
KOW-zet   of victor

☐ **Deena** Hebrew   divine, goddess-like
                                  or valley

☐ **Edna** Hebrew   pleasure, delight

☐ **Elphaba** recently invented by –
EL-fuh-baa   Gregory Maguire

☐ **Harold** English, Old Norse   powerful army

☐ **Price** English from Welsh   ardor, enthusiasm
            name Rhys

☐ **Rapunzel** English from   rampion or lamb's
               German plant   lettuce

☐ **Roxie** Persian, Greek   dawn, bright,
                                   shining

☐ **Schroeder** German   tailor, beer-porter,
SHRO-der   wine-porter

☐ **Warner** English from   army guard
             German

This list includes references from shows *Les Misérables*, *Dream Girls*, *Hairspray*, *Wicked*, *The Music Man*, *The Book of Mormon*, *Into the Woods*, *Chicago*, *You're a Good Man, Charlie Brown*, and *Legally Blonde*.

CITIES

<u>Popular</u>

☐	**Austin**	English from Latin	great, magnificent
☐	**Boston**	English	Botolph's town
☐	**Cheyenne** SHAI-an	Native American	people of a different language
☐	**Dallas**	Scottish, English	the valley meadows
☐	**London**	English from Latin	unconfirmed
☐	**Orlando**	Italian, Spanish	famous throughout the land
☐	**Paris**	Greek, Latin, French	possibly a tribe of Gaul or the lover
☐	**Phoenix**	Greek	dark red
☐	**Savannah**	Spanish	large, grassy plain
☐	**Sydney**	English, French	wide meadow, Saint Denis

<u>Uncommon</u>

☐	**Acadia**	French, Greek	idyllic place
☐	**Brighton**	English	bright town
☐	**Bristol**	Old English	place at the bridge
☐	**Cairo**	Arabic	the strong, victorious, the conqueror
☐	**Halifax**	Old English	secluded spot, nook of land
☐	**Milan**	Slavic	gracious, dear
☐	**Odessa**	possibly Greek	long journey
☐	**Oslo**	Norwegian	meadow at the foot of a hill
☐	**Verona**	Italian	true image
☐	**Vienna**	Latin	forest stream

COLORFUL

Popular

- ☐ **Bleu** — French — blue
- ☐ **Bruno** — Old German — brown
- ☐ **Coral** — English, Spanish — pink-orange
- ☐ **Crimson** — English — deep red
- ☐ **Gray** — English — grey
- ☐ **Marigold** — English — golden flower
- ☐ **Olive** — English from Latin — dark yellow-green
- ☐ **Raven** — Old English — black
- ☐ **Scarlett** — English — bright red
- ☐ **Sienna** — English, Italian — orange-red

<u>Uncommon</u>

☐	**Blaine**	Old Irish	yellow
☐	**Burgundy**	French	dark red
☐	**Chartreuse**	French	yellow-green
☐	**Cyan** SAI-an	English	greenish blue
☐	**Greige**	French	blend of gray and beige
☐	**Ianthe** eye-ANN-thee or ee-ANN-thee	Greek	violet flower
☐	**Lavender**	English	purple flower
☐	**Saffron**	Old French	golden yellow
☐	**Slate**	English	deep gray
☐	**Viridian**	English from Latin	blue-green

COTTAGECORE

Popular

☐	**Aspen**	Old English	aspen tree
☐	**August**	German from Latin	exalted, venerable, great
☐	**Beckett**	English	stream, brook, or beehive
☐	**Elliott**	English from Hebrew	my God is Yahweh
☐	**Jonah**	Hebrew	dove
☐	**Juniper**	English from Latin	young, evergreen, produce
☐	**Magnolia**	English from French surname	Magnol's flower
☐	**Meadow**	Old English	meadow
☐	**Nora**	English from Latin or Old French	shonor, esteem or meaning unknown
☐	**Sawyer**	English	sawer of wood

<u>Uncommon</u>

☐	**Acacia** a-KAY-sha	Greek	thorn, point
☐	**Clarabelle**	Latin	bright + beautiful
☐	**Cricket**	English from Greek	a Christian
☐	**Forrest**	English	lives near a forest
☐	**Gretel**	German, Danish, Norwegian	pearl
☐	**Ingrid**	Old Norse	Ing is beautiful
☐	**Lark**	English	songbird
☐	**Linus**	Greek	flax
☐	**Phineas**	English from Egyptian or Hebrew	Nubian or serpent's mouth
☐	**Rufus**	Latin	red-haired

COUNTRY COOL

Popular

	Name	Origin	Meaning
☐	**Bryce**	Scottish	speckled, freckled
☐	**Delilah**	Hebrew	delicate
☐	**Gage**	French	pledge, oath
☐	**Hank**	German, from Henry	home ruler
☐	**Harper**	English	harpist, minstrel
☐	**Jace**	Greek or Hebrew	to heal or Lord is salvation
☐	**Presley**	Old English	from the priest's meadow
☐	**Ruby**	Latin	deep, red precious stone
☐	**Sadie**	Hebrew	princess
☐	**Wyatt**	Old English	brave at war

<u>Uncommon</u>

☐	**Brock**	English	badger
☐	**Colson**	English or French	son of Nicholas or swarthy, charcoal
☐	**Dolly**	English	gift of God
☐	**Dutton**	English	hill town, Dodd's town
☐	**Nell**	English	bright, shining one
☐	**Reba**	Hebrew	to tie firmly, fourth
☐	**Rowdy**	American	loud, spirited
☐	**Tennessee**	Cherokee	place name
☐	**Thelma**	English	unknown
☐	**Waylon**	Old English	land by the road

DARK ACADEMIA

Popular

☐	**Alistair** AL-iss-tur	English from Scottish	defending men
☐	**Bronwen**	Welsh	white breast, blessed
☐	**Dahlia**	Swedish	Dahl's flower
☐	**Gideon**	Hebrew	feller, hewer
☐	**Ivan**	Slavic version of John	God is gracious
☐	**Jasper**	Persian	bringer of treasure
☐	**Kane**	Old Irish	battle, warrior
☐	**Lilith**	Assyrian	of the night
☐	**Persephone** pr-SEH-fuh-nee	Greek	to destroy
☐	**Sybil**	Greek	prophetess

<u>Uncommon</u>

☐	**Ashby**	English	ash tree farm
☐	**Desdemona**	Greek	ill-fated, unlucky
☐	**Lorimer**	Scottish, Old French	bridle maker
☐	**Morrigan**	Irish	great queen or demon queen
☐	**Morwenna**	Welsh	maiden, waves of the sea
☐	**Nyx**	Greek	night
☐	**Poe**	English	peacock
☐	**Thisbe**	Greek	unknown, lover from Greek mythology
☐	**Wednesday**	English	Woden's day
☐	**Wisteria**	English	Wistar's flower

DINOS & DRAGONS

Popular

☐ **Cera**	Hebrew, inspired by Triceratops	princess, noblewoman
☐ **Devon**	English, dragon in *Quest for Camelot*	place name
☐ **Draco**	Old Norse, Old English	dragon
☐ **Drake**	Old English	dragon, serpent
☐ **Maia**	Greek, inspired by Maiasaura	great, mother
☐ **Ovi**	Latin, inspired by Oviraptor	sheep
☐ **Rex**	Latin, inspired by Tyrannosaurus Rex	king
☐ **Spike**	English	thin, sharp piece of metal
☐ **Titan**	English	Greek mythology term or one who is gigantic in size or power
☐ **Tyra**	Old Norse, inspired by Tyrannosaurus Rex	God of battle or thunder warrior

Uncommon

☐ **Alvara**	inspired by Alvarezsaurus	Alvarez's lizard
☐ **Brach**	German, inspired by Brachiosaurus	possibly pastureland or a female hound
☐ **Hesper**	Greek, inspired by a dinosaur bird	evening
☐ **Jobaria**	genus of Sauropod dinosaurs	mythical creature
☐ **Maleficent**	English from Latin	harmful
☐ **Pelora**	Greek, inspired by Pelorosaurus	monstrous lizard
☐ **Ryu** REE-yu	Japanese	dragon
☐ **Stegg**	Greek, inspired by Stegosaurus	roof lizard or covered lizard
☐ **Wyvern** WY-vern	English from Latin	mythical dragon with two legs and two wings, pointed tail
Xeno	Greek, inspired by multiple dinosaurs	foreigner, guest

ETHEREAL

Popular

☐	**Aisling** ASH-ling or ASH-leen	Irish	dream, vision
☐	**Aurora**	Latin	dawn
☐	**Callum**	Scottish from Latin	dove
☐	**Cassius** KA-see-uhs or KASH-uhs	Latin	empty, vain
☐	**Celeste**	Latin	of the sea, heavenly
☐	**Nova**	Latin	new
☐	**Orion**	Greek	boundary, limit
☐	**Shiloh**	Hebrew	tranquil
☐	**Skye**	Scottish or Old Norse	place name or cloud island
☐	**Wren**	English	small bird

<u>Uncommon</u>

☐	**Ambrosia** am-BRO-see-a or am-BRO-zhuh	Latin	immortal
☐	**Arwen**	Invented	noble maiden
☐	**Cosima** KAW-zee-ma or KO-zee-ma	Italian from Greek	order, decency, universe, beauty
☐	**Demetrius**	Greek	belonging to Demeter
☐	**Endellion** ehn-DEHL-ee-an	Latin form of a Cornish or Welsh name	place and saint name
☐	**Hercules**	Greek	glory of Hera
☐	**Nolwenn**	Breton	holy one from Noyal
☐	**Perseus**	Greek	to destroy
☐	**Titania** ti-TAHN-yah	Latin	possibly of the Titans
☐	**Zenith**	English	the highest point or state, peak

FIRE & ICE

Popular

☐	**Aidan**	Old Irish	little fire
☐	**Bianca**	Italian	white
☐	**Blaze**	English	strongly burning fire
☐	**Brant**	Old Norse	sword, fiery torch
☐	**Ember**	English	small piece of burning or glowing coal
☐	**Isolde** ih-ZOL-duh or ee-SOL-duh	German	ice battle, ice ruler
☐	**January**	English from Latin	Roman god Janus
☐	**Keegan**	Old Irish	fire, son of Aodhagán
☐	**Neve** NEEV	Irish, Latin	snow, bright
☐	**Winter**	English	winter season

<u>Uncommon</u>

☐	**Albus**	Latin	white, bright
☐	**Conley**	Old Irish	constant fire, wise
☐	**Fiamma** FYAM-ma	Italian	flame
☐	**Hestia**	Greek	hearth, fireside
☐	**Icelyn**	English	invented
☐	**Lumi**	Finnish	snow
☐	**Nevada**	Spanish	snow-capped
☐	**Olwen** OL-wehn	Welsh	white footprint
☐	**Seraphina**	Latin, Hebrew	fiery
☐	**Whitaker**	Old English	white field

FOOD & DRINK

Popular

☐ **Basil**   Greek   king

☐ **Brie**   French   region in France

☐ **Clementine**   French from Latin   merciful, gentle

☐ **Ginger**   English from Latin   virginal, pure

☐ **Madeleine**   French   of Magdala

☐ **Maple**   Old English   maple tree

☐ **Nori**   Japanese   ceremony, rites

☐ **Poppy**   Old English   red flower

☐ **Reuben**   Hebrew   behold, a son

☐ **Sage**   English from Latin   to be wise

<u>Uncommon</u>

☐	**Barley**	Old English	of barley, barley store
☐	**Cayenne** KAI-en	Old Tupi	hot pepper
☐	**Cinnamon**	English from Greek, Latin	true cinnamon
☐	**Fennel**	Old English from Latin	hay
☐	**Hershey**	Norman	from Hercé
☐	**Honey**	English	honey
☐	**Nettle**	Old English	person from a place overgrown with nettles
☐	**Pepper**	Old English from Latin	pepper spice
☐	**Rye**	Old English	possibly at the island or person who worked with rye
☐	**Tamarind** TA-mr-uhnd	Arabic	Indian date

GROUNDED

Popular

☐	**Cole**	Old English	charcoal, swarthy, coal black
☐	**Craig**	Scottish, Gaelic	person living near the crags or rocks
☐	**Emerald**	English from Greek	green precious stone
☐	**Gaia**	Greek	earth
☐	**Gemma**	Italian	precious stone
☐	**Harlow**	English	rock army, rock hill
☐	**Jade**	Spanish	stone of the side
☐	**Mason**	English from French	stoneworker
☐	**Rocco**	Italian	rest, repose
☐	**Terra**	Latin	land, earth

<u>Uncommon</u>

☐	**Carrick**	Gaelic	rocky place
☐	**Clifford**	Old English	ford by a cliff
☐	**Dunstan**	Old English	brown stone
☐	**Flint**	Old English	flint
☐	**Garnet**	Middle English	dark red gemstone
☐	**Petra**	Greek	stone
☐	**Rochelle**	French	little rock
☐	**Stein**	German, Old Norse	stone
☐	**Wystan** WIS-tuhn	Old English	battle stone
☐	**Zuriel**	Hebrew	God is my rock

INTERNATIONAL

Popular

	Name	Origin	Meaning
☐	**Amelia**	English from Germanic	vigorous, brave, unceasing, work
☐	**Carlos**	Spanish, Portuguese from Germanic	free person
☐	**Elena**	Spanish, Italian, German, Greek	torch, light
☐	**Emilio**	Spanish, Italian from Latin	rival
☐	**Layla**	Arabic	night
☐	**Luna**	Latin	moon
☐	**Mateo**	Spanish from Hebrew	gift of God
☐	**Nico**	Greek	victory of the people
☐	**Nina**	Russian, Italian, Spanish, English, French, and more	varies depending on the root name
☐	**Sebastian**	Latin from Greek	venerable, from Sebastia

Uncommon

☐	**Anton**	German, Russian, Dutch	from Antium
☐	**Avi**	Hebrew	father of many
☐	**Faris**	Arabic	rider, knight
☐	**Ilari** EE-la-ree	Latin, Greek	cheerful
☐	**Leif** LAYF	Old Norse	descendant, heir
☐	**Rosaria**	Spanish, Italian	rosary
☐	**Simona**	French from Hebrew	hearing, listening
☐	**Tarik**	Arabic	visitor, to knock
☐	**Uma** OO-ma	Sanskrit	flax, tranquility, splendor, fame
☐	**Ziva**	Hebrew	bright, radiant

LITERARY

Popular

☐	**Allan**	Irish, English, Scottish, French	handsome, or little rock
☐	**Angela**	Greek, Latin	messenger of God
☐	**Colin**	Scottish	puppy
☐	**Frank**	English from Old German	Frenchman, free person
☐	**Gwendolen**	Welsh	white ring, blessed, loop
☐	**Holden**	Old English	deep valley
☐	**Josephine**	French	he will add
☐	**Oliver**	Latin	olive tree
☐	**Ruth**	Hebrew	friend
☐	**Viola**	Latin	violet

This list includes references from books, plays, and authors Edgar Allan Poe, Maya Angelou, *Romancing Mister Bridgerton*, L. Frank Baum, *The Importance of Being Earnest*, *The Catcher in the Rye*, *Little Women*, *Oliver Twist*, *A Raisin in the Sun*, and *Twelfth Night*.

<u>Uncommon</u>

☐ **Agatha**   Greek   good

☐ **Aslan**   Turkish   lion

☐ **Feyre**   English   fair, beautiful

☐ **Gatsby**   English from Old   farm or settlement on a
                    Norse Gaddesby   hill or spur

☐ **Heathcliff**   English   heath near a cliff

☐ **Holmes**   English, Old Norse   living by a small island
                                             or a near a holly tree

☐ **Katniss**   English   aquatic plant Sagittaria

☐ **Langston**   Old English   long stone

☐ **Winifred**   Old English, Welsh   friend of peace

☐ **Zora**   Slavic   dawn

This list includes references from books and authors Agatha Christie, *The Chronicles of Narnia*, *A Court of Thorns and Roses*, *The Great Gatsby*, *Wuthering Heights*, *Sherlock Holmes*, *The Hunger Games*, Langston Hughes, *Mary Poppins*, and Zora Neale Hurston.

LOVE (IS ALL YOU NEED)

Popular

☐ **Amanda**	Latin	lovable, worthy of love
☐ **Caleb**	Hebrew	dog, whole heart
☐ **Cara**	Latin, Italian, Irish, Spanish	beloved and friend
☐ **Davis**	English from Hebrew	beloved
☐ **Esme** EHZ-may	French	loved
☐ **Juliet**	English from Latin	youthful, downy-bearded, sky father
☐ **Kevin**	Irish	handsome, beloved
☐ **Mabel**	Latin	lovable
☐ **Tristan**	Celtic	sadness or noise
☐ **Valentino**	Latin	strength, health

<u>Uncommon</u>

☐	**Arrow**	English	a missile shot from a bow
☐	**Caradoc** kaa-RA-dawk	Welsh	love
☐	**Darla**	English	darling
☐	**Eros** eh-ROWS	Greek	love, desire
☐	**Frigg**	Norse	beloved
☐	**Kerensa**	Cornish	love
☐	**Lev**	Hebrew, Russian	heart and lion
☐	**Lovely**	English	beautiful, charming
☐	**Lysander**	Greek	liberator
☐	**Priya**	Sanskrit	beloved

MAIN CHARACTER ENERGY

Popular

☐	**Archer**	English from French	bowman
☐	**Dominic**	Latin	belonging to the Lord
☐	**Esmerelda**	Old Spanish, Old French	emerald
☐	**Genevieve**	English from French	tribe woman
☐	**Lucille**	French from Latin	light
☐	**Matilda**	English from Germanic	strength in battle
☐	**Maximus**	Latin	greatest
☐	**Montgomery**	Norman French	Gumarich's mountain
☐	**Selah**	Hebrew	praise, musical pause
☐	**Valeria**	Latin	to be strong, healthy

Uncommon

☐ **Arcturus**	Greek	guardian of the bear
☐ **Cressida**	English from Greek	gold
☐ **Daughtry**	English from Norman French	high bank
☐ **Evren**	Turkish	the universe
☐ **Luxe**	English	luxurious, elegant
☐ **Quentin**	Latin	fifth
☐ **Rhiannon**	Welsh	great or divine queen
☐ **Sonder**	invented by John Koenig	the realization that each random passerby is living a life as vivid and complex as your own
☐ **Sperry**	English from Old Norse	unknown
☐ **Wolfgang**	Old German	wolf path, way

MIDDLE SPOT

Popular

☐	**Asher**	Hebrew	happy, blessed
☐	**Belle**	French (or short form of Isabelle)	beautiful
☐	**Claire**	French from Latin	bright, clear
☐	**Jane**	English from Hebrew	God is gracious
☐	**Jules**	French from Latin, Greek	youthful, downy-bearded, sky father
☐	**Lynn**	Welsh	lake
☐	**Marie**	French from Hebrew or Egyptian	bitter, beloved, wished for child, rebelliousness
☐	**Patrick**	Latin	nobleman, patrician
☐	**Reed**	Old English	red-haired, ruddy, plant name
☐	**Summer**	English	summer

<u>Uncommon</u>

☐	**Corinne**	French from Greek	maiden
☐	**Danger**	English from Old French	possibility of suffering harm or injury
☐	**Delphine**	French from Greek	of Delphi, womb
☐	**Estelle**	Old French	star
☐	**Fernando**	Spanish, Portuguese	adventurous, bold journey
☐	**Maureen**	Irish version of Mary	bitter, beloved, wished for child, rebelliousness
☐	**Nadine**	French from Russian	hope
☐	**Onyx**	English from Greek	fingernail or claw, gemstone
☐	**Valkyrie** VAL-keh-ree	Old Norse	chooser of the slain
☐	**Xavier** egs-ZAY-vyur or ZAY-vyur	Basque	the new house

MYTHOLOGICAL

<u>Popular</u>

☐	**Apollo**	Greek	possibly strength or to destroy
☐	**Athena**	Greek	possibly from Athens
☐	**Conall**	Old Irish	rule of a wolf, hound, or dog
☐	**Cynthia**	Greek	woman from Cynthus
☐	**Damon**	English from Greek	to tame
☐	**Erik**	Old Norse	ever ruler
☐	**Flora**	Latin	flower
☐	**Hector**	Greek	holding fast
☐	**Helen**	Greek	torch, shining light
☐	**Odin**	Old Norse	inspiration, rage, fury

<u>Uncommon</u>

☐	**Ariadne** ar-ee-AD-nee	Greek	most holy
☐	**Astraea** uh-STRAY-ah	Greek	star
☐	**Fauna**	Latin	possibly to befriend
☐	**Frey**	Old Norse	lord
☐	**Juno**	Latin	possibly young
☐	**Minerva**	Latin, Etruscan	intellect
☐	**Ragnar**	Old Norse	counsel warrior
☐	**Romulus**	Latin	citizen of Rome
☐	**Solveig** SOOL-vay	Old Norse	sun strength
☐	**Theseus**	Greek	possibly to set, to place

NATURE ADJACENT

Popular

☐	**Adler**	German	eagle
☐	**Arlo**	Old English	fortified hill
☐	**Brent**	English from Celtic	hill
☐	**Chloe**	Greek	green shoot
☐	**Hadley**	Old English	heather field
☐	**Landon**	Old English	long hill
☐	**Laurel**	English from Latin	laurel tree
☐	**Nash**	English	at the ash tree
☐	**Shirley**	Old English	bright clearing or meadow
☐	**Wesley**	Old English	western meadow or clearing

<u>Uncommon</u>

☐	**Ainsley**	English from Scottish	solitary meadow or clearing
☐	**Clive**	Old English	cliff dweller
☐	**Elowen** EL-oh-win	Cornish	elm tree
☐	**Lochlan** LOK-luhn	Scottish	land of the lakes, land of the Vikings
☐	**Murphy**	Irish	sea battle
☐	**Perry**	English	pear tree
☐	**Pomona**	Latin	fruit tree
☐	**Vance**	Old English	marsh
☐	**Vespera**	Latin	of the evening
☐	**Yolanda**	Spanish from Latin and Greek	violet

NICKNAMES

<u>Popular</u>

☐	**Ari**	Hebrew	lion of God
☐	**Bobby**	English from German	bright fame
☐	**Charlie**	French from German	free person
☐	**Elsie**	Hebrew	God is my oath
☐	**Leni**	Greek, German, Latin	light
☐	**Millie**	English or German	gentle strength or strong in work
☐	**Ollie**	Latin	olive tree
☐	**Sonny**	English	son
☐	**Tilly**	English from Germanic	strength in battle
☐	**Wally**	German	commander of the army

<u>Uncommon</u>

☐ **Birdie**	English	bird
☐ **Bunty**	English or Scottish	lamb or plump
☐ **Lettie**	English from Latin	joy, gladness
☐ **Lonny**	English from Spanish or Italian	noble and ready
☐ **Marty**	Latin	warlike, of Mars
☐ **Minnie**	German and others	will, desire, helmet, protection
☐ **Ori**	Hebrew	my light
☐ **Ricky**	German	powerful leader
☐ **Winnie**	Old English, Welsh	blessed peacemaking, friend of peace
☐ **Ziggy**	German	victorious protection

OCCUPATIONAL

Popular

☐	**Bailey**	English	bailiff
☐	**Carter**	English	transporter of goods by cart
☐	**Cooper**	English	barrel maker
☐	**Miller**	English	one who grinds grain, works in a mill
☐	**Piper**	English	pipe or flute player
☐	**Porter**	English from French	doorkeeper
☐	**Saylor**	German, French, English	ropemaker, sailor, or acrobat
☐	**Spencer**	English	steward
☐	**Taylor**	English	tailor
☐	**Walker**	English	cloth walker

<u>Uncommon</u>

☐	**Brewer**	English	maker of ale or beer
☐	**Chandler**	English from French	candle maker or candle seller
☐	**Draper**	English	cloth merchant
☐	**Fisher**	English from German	fisherman
☐	**Fletcher**	English from French	maker of arrows
☐	**Mercer**	French	storekeeper or merchant
☐	**Smith**	English	blacksmith
☐	**Thatcher**	English	roof hatcher
☐	**Wainwright**	English	maker of wagons
☐	**Webb**	English	weaver

OLD MONEY

Popular

	Name	Origin	Meaning
☐	**Alfred**	Old English	elf counsel
☐	**Cecilia**	Latin	blind
☐	**Dawson**	English	son of David
☐	**Everett**	English from German	brave boar
☐	**Franklin**	English	free person
☐	**Jacqueline** JAK-e-lin or JAK-e-leen	French	supplanter
☐	**Kenneth**	Scottish, Irish	handsome, born of fire
☐	**Margaret**	Greek	pearl
☐	**Otto**	German	wealth, fortune
☐	**Palmer**	English from Latin	pilgrim, palm tree

<u>Uncommon</u>

☐ **Corliss** Old English free from anxiety,
KOR-les   carefree

☐ **Della** German noble

☐ **Fitzgerald** Irish, Scottish from son of Gerald
Norman

☐ **Odette** French from wealth, fortune
German

☐ **Prentice** English apprentice

☐ **Radcliffe** Old English red cliff

☐ **Romilly** English, French person from
from Latin Romilly

☐ **Sinclair** Scottish from a Norman
French town named
Saint Clair

☐ **Vanderbilt** Dutch, German from the low hill

☐ **Winthrop** Old English Wigmund's village

PIRATE

Popular

☐	**Atlas**	Greek	possibly enduring, word name
☐	**Casper**	Dutch from Persian and Latin	treasure
☐	**Chase**	English, Old French	chase, hunt
☐	**Decker**	German	roofer
☐	**Hartley**	Old English	male deer, woodland, clearing
☐	**Jack**	English	God is gracious
☐	**Polly**	English from Molly	bitter, beloved, wished for child, rebelliousness
☐	**Rachel**	Hebrew	ewe
☐	**Roger**	German	famous spear
☐	**Sparrow**	Middle English	sparrow

<u>Uncommon</u>

☐ **Beryl** BEHR-el — English from Greek — sea-green precious stone

☐ **Bucky** — Old English — male deer or rabbit

☐ **Captain** — Latin — head, leader

☐ **Kenza** — Arabic — treasure

☐ **Landry** — French from Germanic — ruler, king

☐ **Lassie** — English, Scottish — little girl

☐ **Maroon** — English, French — stranded in an isolated place, color name

☐ **Marquis** maar-KEE or MAA-kwuhs — English from Old French — march, borderland, nobleman

☐ **Skipper** — Middle Dutch — boatman, captain

☐ **Tide** — Old English — time

PLAYFUL & FUN

Popular

☐	**Caden**	English, Irish, Welsh or invented	possibly battle or warrior
☐	**Eli** EE-lie	Hebrew	ascension, uplifted
☐	**Grayson**	English	son of the steward
☐	**Hugo**	German, Latin from Hugh	mind, thought, intellect, spirit
☐	**Maisie**	Scottish	pearl
☐	**Melody**	English from Greek	song
☐	**Paige**	English	young servant or helper
☐	**Tessa**	Greek	to harvest
☐	**Wiley**	Old English	willow meadow
☐	**Willa**	German	will, helmet or protection

<u>Uncommon</u>

☐ **Boden** — Sanskrit, variation of Bodhi — enlightenment

☐ **Hall** — Old English — one who works at a manor or hall

☐ **Etta** — French, German, and more — home ruler

☐ **Fox** — English — animal name

☐ **Indie** — Sanskrit, short form of India — body of trembling water, river

☐ **Jago** JAY-goh or YAH-goh — Cornish and Spanish version of Jacob — supplanter

☐ **Jorie** — medieval variation of Margaret, taken from Marjorie — pearl

☐ **Oona** — Old Irish, from Una — lamb

☐ **Tolliver** TAHL-i-vur — English from Italian — iron cutter

☐ **Veda** VAY-duh — Sanskrit — knowledge

PURITAN

Popular

☐	**Charity**	English from Latin	generous love
☐	**Christian**	English and Greek from Latin	a Christian
☐	**Faith**	English from Latin	to trust
☐	**Felicity**	English from Latin	happiness, good fortune
☐	**Grace**	English from Latin	favor, blessing
☐	**Hope**	Old English	the virtue of hope
☐	**Jenning**	Hebrew, variation of John	God is gracious
☐	**Justice**	English from Old French	judge, officer of justice
☐	**Prudence**	English from French	prudent, wise, skilled
☐	**Truly**	Old English	faithfully

<u>Uncommon</u>

☐ **Beloved**   English   dearly loved

☐ **Constance**   English from Latin   steadfastness

☐ **Mercy**   English, French   compassion

☐ **Providence**   English   divine care or direction

☐ **Reason**   English   statement offered in explanation

☐ **Temperance**   English   moderation

☐ **Thankful**   English   conscious of benefit received

☐ **Verity**   English from Latin   truth, real

☐ **Virtue**   English from Latin   valor, worth

☐ **Wrestling**   Old English   sport of grappling with an opponent

QUIRKY & COOL

<u>Popular</u>

☐ **Astrid**	Scandinavian	divinely beautiful
☐ **Daphne**	Greek	laurel tree
☐ **Ezra**	Hebrew	help
☐ **Knox**	Scottish	round hill
☐ **Irving**	Scottish	green river, fresh water, sea friend
☐ **Milo**	German, Latin	soldier, merciful, beloved
☐ **Phoebe**	Greek	bright, radiant, pure
☐ **Quinn**	Irish	wise, descending from Conn
☐ **Winston**	English	joyful stone or wine's town
☐ **Zoe** ZOH-ee	Greek	life

<u>Uncommon</u>

☐	**Cassiopeia** ka-see-OW-pee-uh	Greek	cassia juice
☐	**Digby**	English, Norse	town or farm by the ditch
☐	**Early**	English	before due time or date
☐	**Hester**	Hebrew, Persian	star, myrtle leaf
☐	**Imogen** IM-a-jehn	Celtic	maiden
☐	**Mavis**	French	songbird
☐	**Nigel**	Celtic	dark, black-haired
☐	**Ridley**	English	reed/wood clearing
☐	**Wilbur**	Old German	resolute, brilliant
☐	**Velma**	German	will, helmet or protector

SCIENTISTS

Popular

☐	**Ada**	German	noble, of nobility
☐	**Barry**	Irish	fair-haired, fair-topped
☐	**Carl**	German, Scandinavian	free person
☐	**Ellen**	English variation of Helen	torch, shining light
☐	**Irene**	Greek	peace
☐	**James**	English from Hebrew	holder of heel or supplanter
☐	**Mario**	Spanish, Italian	manly, warlike
☐	**Rosalind**	Old German or Latin	soft horse or beautiful rose
☐	**Samuel**	Hebrew	name of God
☐	**Virginia**	Latin	maid, virgin

This list includes references to the scientists Ada Lovelace, Barry Paw, Carl Woese, Ellen Ochoa, Irene Uchida, James Chadwick, Mario J. Molina, Rosalind Franklin, Samuel Morse, and Virginia Holsinger.

<u>Uncommon</u>

☐	**Carver**	Middle English	one who cuts or carves
☐	**Curie** KYU-ree	Old French	stable
☐	**Darwin**	Old English	dear friend
☐	**Inge** ING-eh	Scandinavian, German	possibly ancestor or guarded by Ing
☐	**Kepler**	German	hooded cloak
☐	**Mildred**	Old English	gentle strength
☐	**Newton**	Old English	new town
☐	**Niels** NEHLS	Danish variation of Nicholas	victory of the people
☐	**Percy**	Norman	place name from Percy-en-Auge
☐	**Ynes** ee-NEHS	Spanish variation of Agnes, alternative to Ines	pure, virginal

This list includes references to the scientists George Washington Carver, Marie Curie, Charles Darwin, Inge Lehmann, Johannes Kepler, Mildred Dresselhaus, Isaac Newton, Niels Bohr, Percy Lavon Julian, and Ynes Mexia.

SOPHISTICATION

Popular

☐	**Anastasia**	Greek	resurrection
☐	**Archibald**	Scottish from German	bold, brave
☐	**Bennett**	English from Latin	blessed
☐	**Cameron**	Scottish	crooked nose
☐	**Desmond**	Irish	from South Munster
☐	**Eloise** EHL-o-eez	Old French	healthy, whole
☐	**Lawrence**	English from Latin	from Laurentum
☐	**Natalia**	Polish, Italian, Spanish from Latin	Christmas Day
☐	**Soren**	Danish from Latin	stern
☐	**Walter**	German	power of the army

Uncommon

☐	**Bijou** bee-ZHOO	French	jewel
☐	**Emmeline**	Old French	unceasing, vigorous, brave
☐	**Hastings**	English	possibly from the name Hasten
☐	**Ludivine** LOO-dih-veen	French	friend to the people
☐	**Ottilie**	German, French	heritage, wealth, fortune
☐	**Pierce**	English, French from Greek	rock or stone
☐	**Rosamund**	English from Old German	horse protection
☐	**Rupert**	German	bright fame
☐	**Sophronia**	Greek	sensible, self-controlled
☐	**Townsend**	English	edge of town

SPIRITUAL

Popular

☐ **Abraham** Hebrew father of many

☐ **Bodhi** Sanskrit enlightenment
BO-dee

☐ **Celine** French from Latin heavenly

☐ **Destiny** English destiny, fate

☐ **Elijah** Hebrew my God is Yahweh

☐ **Genesis** Greek origin, source, beginning

☐ **Halo** English from Greek luminous disc or ring

☐ **Nevaeh** English, invented heaven spelled backwards
nuh-VAY-ah

☐ **Saint** Latin sacred, holy

☐ **Zion** Hebrew highest point, stronghold, fortress

<u>Uncommon</u>

☐	**Angelica**	English, Italian, Russian from Latin	angelic
☐	**Aziz** a-ZEEZ	Arabic	powerful, respected, beloved
☐	**Celestino**	Latin	of the sky, heavenly
☐	**Karma**	Sanskrit	action, destiny, fate
☐	**Hosanna**	Hebrew	deliver us
☐	**Mitchell**	English from Hebrew	who is like God?
☐	**Muhammed**	Arabic	praiseworthy
☐	**Parisa**	Persian	like a fairy
☐	**Shoshana** sho-SHAH-nah	Hebrew	lily
☐	**Trinity**	Latin	triad

SPORTY

Popular

☐	**Brady**	Irish	descendant of Brádach, spirited
☐	**Casey**	Irish	descendant of Cathassach, vigilant
☐	**Clark**	Old English	cleric, scribe
☐	**Colt**	Middle English	keeper of horses
☐	**Emmett**	English from German	universal, whole
☐	**Jordan**	English from Hebrew	flowing down
☐	**Kyler**	Dutch or invented	bowman, archer
☐	**Lane**	English	lane, path
☐	**Mia**	Italian, Scandinavian	mine or bitter
☐	**Serena**	Latin	tranquil, serene

Uncommon

☐	**Ace**	English from Latin	one, unity, highest rank
☐	**Axel**	Scandinavian	father of peace
☐	**Blade**	Old English	leaf of a plant, word name
☐	**Curry**	Irish	from Comhraidhe
☐	**Danica**	Slavic	morning star, Venus
☐	**Hooper**	English	hoop-maker
☐	**Kerrigan**	Irish	descendant of Ciaragán
☐	**Olympia**	Greek	from Mount Olympus
☐	**Rawley**	English	red woodland clearing
☐	**Venus**	Latin	love, desire

STEPH'S FAVORITES

Popular

☐	**Banks**	English	one who lives near the hillside or riverbank
☐	**Beckham**	English	Becca's homestead or homestead by the stream
☐	**Cora**	Greek	maiden
☐	**Florence**	Latin	prosperous, flourishing
☐	**Lara**	Russian, from Larissa	citadel
☐	**Lennox**	Scottish	place of elms
☐	**Logan**	Scottish	little hollow
☐	**Margot**	French	pearl
☐	**Sylvie**	French from Latin	from the forest
☐	**Tate**	English from Old Norse	cheerful

Uncommon

☐ **Araceli** a-ra-SEH-lee	Spanish	altar of the sky
☐ **Barlowe**	English	barley hill or clearing
☐ **Carys** KAHR-is	Welsh	love
☐ **Cypress**	English from Greek	evergreen, coniferous tree
☐ **Greer**	Scottish from Latin	alert, watchful
☐ **Renata**	Latin	reborn
☐ **Roscoe**	Norse	deer wood, forest
☐ **Selwyn** SEHL-win	Old English	manor friend
☐ **Signe** SING-neh, SIG-nee, or SEE-neh	Scandinavian	new victory
☐ **Vermilion**	French	bright, rich, deep red color

TOUGH GALS & GUYS

Popular

☐	**Aaliyah** ah-LEE-ah	Arabic	high, lofty, sublime
☐	**Amari**	Sanskrit, Hebrew, African	possibly goddess, eternal, grace, courage
☐	**Gavin**	Celtic	white hawk
☐	**Gunner**	Old Norse	warrior
☐	**Maverick**	English	independent, nonconformist
☐	**Naomi**	Hebrew	pleasantness
☐	**Raya**	Hebrew or Latin	friend or queen
☐	**Roman**	Latin	from Rome
☐	**Ryder**	Old English	mounted warrior or messenger
☐	**Sloane**	Irish	raider

<u>Uncommon</u>

☐	**Antigone** an-TIG-a-nee	Greek	compared to one's parents, in place of
☐	**Bowie**	Scottish	yellow-haired, blond
☐	**Cleo**	Greek	glory
☐	**Conan**	Irish	little wolf, little hound
☐	**Daya**	Sanskrit or Hebrew	compassionate or bird of prey
☐	**Fallon**	Irish	leader
☐	**Kenzo**	Japanese	healthy, humble, wise
☐	**Lorcan**	Irish	little fierce one
☐	**Sabre** SAY-br	French	sword
☐	**Zelda**	English from German Griselda	grey battle

TV SHOWS

Popular

☐	**Blair**	Scottish	plain, field, battlefield
☐	**Diane**	French from Latin	divine, goddess
☐	**Elaine**	French from Greek	torch, bright shining light
☐	**Gregory**	English from Greek	watchful, alert, vigilant
☐	**Jason**	Greek	to heal
☐	**Joel**	Hebrew	Yahweh is God
☐	**Leslie**	Scottish	garden of holly
☐	**Lorelai** LAWR-i-lie	German	possibly alluring temptress
☐	**Santana**	Spanish	contraction of Santa Ana
☐	**Titus**	unknown, possibly Latin	title of honor

This list includes references to TV programs *Gossip Girl*, *Cheers*, *Seinfeld*, *House*, *The Good Place*, *The Last of Us*, *Parks and Rec*, *Gilmore Girls*, *Glee*, and *Unbreakable Kimmy Schmidt*.

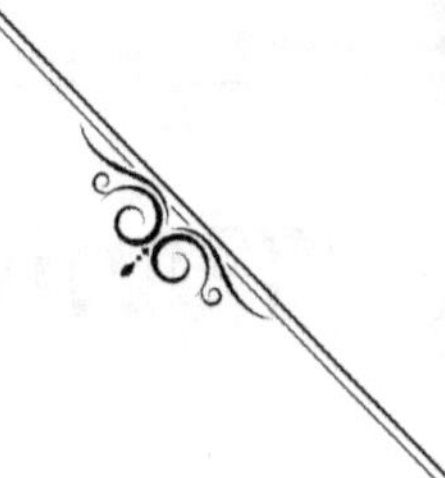

<u>Uncommon</u>

☐ **Buffy**	English from Hebrew	God is my oath
☐ **Calypso** kuh-LIP-sow	Greek	to cover, to conceal
☐ **Crosby**	English, Norse	dweller by the cross
☐ **Daenerys** duh-NEH-ruhs	English	invented, unknown
☐ **Dwight**	Greek from Dionysus or Dutch	white, blond
☐ **Eleven**	Old English	one left (after 10)
☐ **Glenn**	Scottish	valley
☐ **Hyacinth** HAI-uh-snth	Greek	blue larkspur flower
☐ **Rainbow**	English	rainbow
☐ **Sheldon**	English	valley with steep sides

This list includes references to TV programs *Buffy the Vampire Slayer*, *Bluey*, *Parenthood*, *Game of Thrones*, *The Office*, *Stranger Things*, *The Walking Dead*, *Bridgerton*, *Black-ish*, and *The Big Bang Theory*.

TWIN COMBOS

Boy/Boy

Boaz & Riven

Boaz BO-az	Hebrew	swiftness
Riven	English from Norse	to tear down, to split

Declan & Henley

Declan	Old Irish	unknown
Henley	English	high meadow

Frederick & Paxton

Frederick	German	peaceful ruler
Paxton	English	peaceful town

Kiernan & Sylvan

Kiernan KEER-nan	Old Irish from Tiernan	little lord
Sylvan	Latin	wood, forest

Ferris & Westwood

Ferris	Norman	iron
Westwood	Old English	west wood

<u>Girl/Girl</u>

<u>Clarimond & Cornelia</u>

Clarimond Latin, German shining defender

Cornelia Latin horn

<u>Evelyn & Ramona</u>

Evelyn English, French, German desired, island, wished for

Ramona Spanish counsel or advice, protection

<u>Gwyneth & Sabrina</u>

Gwyneth Welsh white, fair, happy

Sabrina Latin from Welsh River Severn unknown

<u>Ivy & Noa</u>

Ivy English climbing plant

Noa Hebrew rest, comfort, or motion

<u>Pippa & Yoli</u>

Pippa English from Greek lover of horses

Yoli Spanish from Latin, Greek violet

Mix

Arden & Ellis

Arden	English from Celtic	high
Ellis	Hebrew, Welsh	my God is Yahweh, kind, benevolent

Arlene & Ira

Arlene	English	unknown
Ira	Hebrew	watchful

Ledger & Lyla

Ledger	Norman, Germanic	spear people
Lyla	Arabic	night

Rhodes & Whitley

Rhodes	Old English	cleared land
Whitley	Old English	white clearing

Rory & Shayna

Rory	Irish	red king
Shayna	Yiddish	beautiful, lovely

WEATHER

Popular

☐	**Elio** EH-lee-oh	Italian, Spanish	sun
☐	**Gale**	English	a very strong wind
☐	**Iris**	Greek	rainbow, flower name
☐	**Keanu** kee-AA-noo	Hawaiian	cool breeze
☐	**Misty**	Old English	water droplets in the air cause a fog
☐	**Neil**	Irish	cloud
☐	**Noelani** no-LA-nee or no-eh-LA-nee	Hawaiian	heavenly mist
☐	**Rain**	Old English	precipitation that falls from the sky
☐	**Solana**	Spanish	sunshine
☐	**Talia**	Hebrew	dew from heaven

<u>Uncommon</u>

☐	**Brisa**	Spanish	breeze, small wind
☐	**Ciel** see-EL	French	sky, heavenly
☐	**Eira** EYE-ra	Welsh	snow
☐	**Guthrie**	Gaelic	windy place
☐	**Indra**	Sanskrit	possesses rain
☐	**Iridiana**	Greek	rainbow
☐	**Raiden**	Japanese	thunder and lightning
☐	**Tempest**	Middle English, Old French	storm, turbulent
☐	**Thora**	Norse	thunder goddess
☐	**Zephyr** ZEHF-r	Greek	west wind

WHIMSICAL WORDS

<u>Popular</u>

☐	**Autumn**	English from Latin	season of fall
☐	**Chance**	English from Latin	luck, fortune
☐	**Cosmo**	English from Greek	order, decency, universe, beauty
☐	**Fern**	Old English	leafy plant with no flowers or seeds
☐	**Harbor**	Old English	give shelter, refuge
☐	**Haven**	Old English	safe place
☐	**June**	English from Latin	month
☐	**Legend**	English from Latin	story about the past
☐	**River**	English	flowing body of water
☐	**Sunday**	English from Latin	sun day

Uncommon

☐	**Afternoon**	English	part of the day between noon and sunset
☐	**Bramble**	Old English	blackberry bush
☐	**Cherish**	English	to hold dear, to treasure
☐	**Evergreen**	English	having foliage that remains green and functional year-round
☐	**Memory**	English from Latin	mindful, remembering
☐	**Meridian**	Latin	midday, noon
☐	**Rooster**	English	roosting bird
☐	**Sonnet**	Italian, Latin	little song, poem
☐	**Velvet**	English	rich, closely woven soft fabric
☐	**Zeal**	English	eagerness, great enthusiasm

EPILOGUE

I HAVE TO PINCH myself most days because my mind has trouble comprehending that my actual job is to help people choose baby names, make videos about names, and write books about names. I get to assist people with a fun and creative—albeit huge—task at one of the most special times in their lives and I do not take that responsibility lightly. In fact, it is a gift.

My best advice when it comes to choosing a name is simple: Pick the name you love and love it loudly and unabashedly. Tell your child how much you cherish their name, tell them the story of how their name came to be, and use their name boldly and with affection as often as possible. My three kids have pretty uncommon names in the United States and they absolutely adore them. Maybe some of it has to do with my profession as a name consultant, but I like to think they feel empowered by their unique monikers.

I cannot promise everyone will love your child's uncommon name as much as you do, but I can promise to continually share different and rare name inspiration so that eventually all names are viewed as special. I cherish meeting someone with a name I've never encountered before, and I love knowing there are still infinite names left to discover. Let's respect everyone's name (and teach our children the same). We owe that to one another.

Do you have a couple of favorites after reading this book? I hope so. And guess what? I LOVE them.

Happy naming,

Steph

FAVORITE NAMES

FAVORITE NAMES

FAVORITE NAMES

FAVORITE NAMES

FAVORITE NAMES

FAVORITE NAMES

NAME INDEX

Ashley	16
Aslan	67
Aspen	48
Astraea	75
Astrid	90
Athena	74
Atlas	84
Atticus	24
Audrey	42
August	48
Augustine	25
Aurelian	27
Aurora	56
Austin	44
Autumn	112
Avella	28
Avi	65
Axel	99
Aziz	97
Bailey	80
Banks	100
Barbie	11
Barley	61
Barlowe	101
Barry	92
Basil	60
Beatrice	41
Beauregard	37
Beckett	48
Beckham	100
Bee	21
Belle	72
Beloved	89

Benjamin	24
Bennett	94
Bentley	38
Bernice	33
Beryl	85
Bianca	58
Bijou	95
Birdie	79
Birgitte	41
Blade	99
Blaine	47
Blair	104
Blake	20
Blanche	28
Blaze	58
Bleu	46
Boaz	106
Bobby	78
Boden	87
Bodhi	96
Bonnie	19
Booker	31
Boris	11
Boston	44
Bowie	103
Brach	55
Brady	98
Bramble	113
Brandon	16
Brant	58
Brenda	10
Brennon	19
Brent	76

Brewer	81
Brian	12
Brie	60
Brighton	45
Brisa	111
Bristol	45
Brittany	16
Brock	51
Bronwen	52
Brooks	38
Bruce	10
Bruno	46
Bryce	50
Bucky	85
Bud	11
Buffy	105
Bunty	79
Burgundy	47
Caden	86
Cairo	45
Caitlin	16
Caleb	68
Calhoun	29
Callum	56
Calvin	38
Calypso	105
Cameron	94
Camilla	40
Captain	85
Cara	68
Caradoc	69
Carl	92
Carlos	64

Cinnamon	61
Claire	72
Clara	22
Clarabelle	49
Clarimond	107
Clark	98
Claude	33
Clementine	60
Cleo	103
Clifford	63
Clive	77
Coast	34
Colby	23
Cole	62
Colin	66
Colson	51
Colt	98
Conall	74
Conan	103
Conley	59
Constance	89
Cooper	80
Cora	100
Coral	46
Cordelia	37
Cordell	11
Corinne	73
Corliss	83
Cornelia	107
Cosette	43
Cosima	57
Cosmo	112
Courtney	22

Cove	35
Craig	62
Crash	29
Cressida	71
Cricket	49
Crimson	46
Crosby	105
Curie	93
Curry	99
Cy	21
Cyan	47
Cynthia	74
Cypress	101
Daenerys	105
Dahlia	52
Dallas	44
Damon	74
Danger	73
Danica	99
Daniel	14
Danny	42
Daphne	90
Darcy	17
Darla	69
Darwin	93
Daughtry	71
David	8
Davis	68
Dawson	82
Daya	103
Dean	20
Debra	8
Decker	84

Declan	106
Deena	43
Delilah	50
Della	83
Delmar	35
Delphine	73
Delroy	29
Demetrius	57
Desdemona	53
Desmond	94
Destiny	96
Devereaux	28
Devon	54
Dewey	15
Dewitt	9
Diana	41
Diane	104
Digby	91
Dior	39
Dolly	51
Dominic	70
Donatello	33
Dorothy	30
Dove	39
Doyle	13
Draco	54
Drake	54
Draper	81
Dunstan	63
Dutton	51
Dwight	105
Dylan	34
Early	91

Edith	23
Edmonia	33
Edna	43
Edward	30
Effie	31
Eira	111
Elaine	104
Eldridge	9
Eleanor	24
Elena	64
Eleven	105
Eli	86
Elijah	96
Elio	110
Elizabeth	40
Ellen	92
Ellington	37
Elliott	48
Ellis	108
Elodie	25
Eloise	94
Elowen	77
Elphaba	43
Elsie	78
Elvin	15
Ember	58
Emerald	62
Emilio	64
Emmanuel	26
Emmeline	95
Emmett	98
Endellion	57
Enoch	31

Erik	74
Ernest	41
Eros	69
Esme	68
Esmerelda	70
Esperanza	27
Estelle	73
Etta	87
Eugenie	41
Evan	42
Evander	36
Evangeline	37
Eve	20
Evelyn	107
Everett	82
Evergreen	113
Evian	39
Evoleth	28
Evren	71
Ezekiel	26
Ezra	90
Faith	88
Fallon	103
Faris	65
Fauna	75
Faye	20
Felicity	88
Felix	30
Fennel	61
Fern	112
Fernando	73
Ferris	106
Feyre	67

Fiamma	59
Finley	22
Finnian	25
Fisher	81
Fitzgerald	83
Fletcher	81
Flint	63
Flora	74
Florence	100
Florian	37
Ford	38
Forrest	49
Fox	87
Francesca	36
Frank	66
Franklin	82
Frederick	106
Frey	75
Frida	33
Frigg	69
Fritz	9
Gabriella	26
Gage	50
Gaia	62
Gale	110
Garnet	63
Gatsby	67
Gavin	102
Gemma	62
Gene	21
Genesis	96
Genevieve	70
George	40

Georgia	32
Gia	19
Gianna	24
Gideon	52
Gilda	11
Ginger	60
Giovanni	26
Glenn	105
Grace	88
Grant	20
Gray	46
Grayson	86
Greer	101
Gregory	104
Greige	47
Gretel	49
Gunner	102
Guthrie	111
Gwendolen	66
Gwyneth	107
Hadley	76
Halifax	45
Hall	87
Halo	96
Hank	50
Hannah	18
Harbor	112
Harley	23
Harlow	62
Harold	43
Harper	50
Harrison	24
Hartley	84

Harvey	19
Hastings	95
Haven	112
Havilah	35
Hazel	30
Heathcliff	67
Heather	14
Hector	74
Helen	74
Henley	106
Henrietta	27
Henry	40
Hercules	57
Hernán	17
Hershel	11
Hershey	61
Hesper	55
Hester	91
Hestia	59
Hickory	29
Hilda	15
Holden	66
Holmes	67
Honey	61
Hooper	99
Hope	88
Horatio	27
Hosanna	97
Hugo	86
Hyacinth	105
Ianthe	47
Ibiza	35
Icelyn	59

Ilari	65
Imogen	91
Indie	87
Indigo	25
Indra	111
Inge	93
Ingrid	49
Ira	108
Irene	92
Iridiana	111
Iris	110
Irving	90
Isaac	22
Isabel	36
Isla	34
Islarose	28
Isolde	58
Ivan	52
Ivy	107
Jace	50
Jack	84
Jackson	32
Jacob	18
Jacqueline	82
Jade	62
Jago	87
James	92
Jane	72
January	58
Jason	104
Jasper	52
Jeffrey	12
Jenna	42

Jennifer	12
Jenning	88
Jeremiah	26
Jeremy	42
Jessica	16
Jobaria	55
Jodie	17
Joel	104
John	8
Jonah	48
Jonathan	18
Jordan	98
Jorie	87
Joseph	16
Josephine	66
Joshua	14
Judd	13
Jude	20
Jules	72
Julian	36
Julie	10
Juliet	68
June	112
Juniper	48
Juno	75
Justice	88
Justin	14
Kai	34
Kane	52
Kara	33
Karma	97
Kate	38
Katniss	67

Kayla	18
Keanu	110
Keegan	58
Keely	15
Kennedy	19
Kenneth	82
Kenza	85
Kenzo	103
Kepler	93
Kerensa	69
Kermit	13
Kerrigan	99
Kerrington	28
Kevin	68
Kia	17
Kiernan	106
Kimberly	12
Kindred	28
Kip	15
Kipling	29
Knox	90
Korbin	19
Kyler	98
Lance	21
Landon	76
Landry	85
Lane	98
Langston	67
Lara	100
Lark	49
Lassie	85
Laurel	76
Lauren	18

Lavender	47
Lawrence	94
Layla	64
Ledger	108
Legend	112
Leif	65
Leland	37
Leni	78
Lennox	100
Leonardo	32
Leonora	33
Leopold	37
Leslie	104
Lettie	79
Lev	69
Levi	38
Lex	9
Liliana	26
Lilibet	41
Lilith	52
Lillian	36
Linda	8
Linus	49
Lisa	10
Lochlan	77
Logan	100
London	44
Lonny	79
Lorcan	103
Lorelai	104
Lorenzo	24
Lorimer	53
Lorne	13

Louis	40
Louise	32
Lourdes	19
Loveday	31
Lovely	69
Lucille	70
Lucy	22
Ludivine	95
Lumi	59
Luna	64
Luxe	71
Lydell	13
Lydia	30
Lyla	108
Lynn	72
Lysander	69
Mabel	68
Macy	38
Madeleine	60
Madison	18
Madonna	9
Magnolia	48
Mahalia	27
Maia	54
Maisie	86
Major	11
Maleficent	55
Maple	60
Marcelino	15
Marcella	37
Maren	23
Margaret	82
Margot	100

Maria	42
Marie	72
Marigold	46
Marina	34
Mario	92
Marjorie	17
Mark	8
Marlow	34
Marnie	13
Maroon	85
Marquis	85
Marty	79
Mary	8
Mason	62
Mateo	64
Matilda	70
Matthew	14
Maureen	73
Maverick	102
Mavis	91
Maximus	70
Maxwell	22
Maybelline	39
Meadow	48
Meghan	41
Melissa	14
Melody	86
Memory	113
Mercedes	38
Mercer	81
Mercy	89
Meridian	113
Mervyn	35

Mia   98
Michael   12
Michelle   12
Milan   45
Mildred   93
Miller   80
Millicent   11
Millie   78
Milo   90
Minerva   75
Minnie   79
Miranda   24
Misty   110
Mitchell   97
Mitzi   13
Molly   42
Mona   15
Montgomery   70
Morgan   18
Morrigan   53
Morris   17
Morwenna   53
Muhammed   97
Murdock   29
Murphy   77
Nadine   73
Nancy   8
Naomi   102
Nash   76
Natalia   94
Nathan   42
Neil   110
Nell   51

Nestor	11
Nettle	61
Nevada	59
Nevaeh	96
Neve	58
Newton	93
Nicholas	24
Nico	64
Nicole	14
Niels	93
Nigel	91
Nike	39
Nina	64
Noa	107
Noelani	110
Nolwenn	57
Nora	48
Nori	60
Nova	56
Nyx	53
Oceana	35
Octavian	27
Odessa	45
Odette	83
Odin	74
Oleander	27
Olive	46
Oliver	66
Olivia	26
Ollie	78
Olwen	59
Olympia	99
Onyx	73

Oona	87
Opal	23
Ophelia	36
Ori	79
Orion	56
Orlando	44
Oscar	30
Oslo	45
Otis	23
Ottilie	95
Otto	82
Ovi	54
Pablo	32
Paige	86
Palmer	82
Paloma	25
Paris	44
Parisa	97
Parker	22
Patricia	10
Patrick	72
Paul	8
Paxton	106
Pearl	34
Pelora	55
Penelope	26
Penn	21
Pepper	61
Percy	93
Permelia	31
Perry	77
Persephone	52
Perseus	57

Peter	32
Petra	63
Philip	41
Philomena	37
Phineas	49
Phoebe	90
Phoenix	44
Pierce	95
Piper	80
Pippa	107
Poe	53
Polly	84
Pomona	77
Poppy	60
Porsche	39
Porter	80
Prentice	83
Presley	50
Price	43
Priscilla	25
Priya	69
Providence	89
Prudence	88
Quentin	71
Quinn	90
Rachel	84
Radcliffe	83
Rae	20
Ragnar	75
Raiden	111
Rain	110
Rainbow	105
Ramona	107

Ransom	31
Raphael	32
Rapunzel	43
Raven	46
Rawley	99
Raya	102
Reason	89
Reba	51
Reed	72
Rembrandt	33
Renata	101
Renton	29
Reuben	60
Rex	54
Rhiannon	71
Rhodes	108
Richard	10
Ricky	79
Ridley	91
Riven	106
River	112
Roark	29
Robert	14
Rocco	62
Rochelle	63
Roger	84
Roman	102
Romilly	83
Romulus	75
Ronald	10
Rooster	113
Rory	108
Rosalie	24

Rosalind	92
Rosamund	95
Rosaria	65
Roscoe	101
Ross	34
Rowdy	51
Roxie	43
Rubin	9
Ruby	50
Rue	21
Rufus	49
Rupert	95
Rusty	17
Ruth	66
Ryan	14
Ryder	102
Rye	61
Ryu	55
Sabre	103
Sabrina	107
Sadie	50
Saffron	47
Sage	60
Saint	96
Sally	17
Samantha	16
Samson	15
Samuel	92
Sandra	8
Sandy	34
Santana	104
Santiago	36
Sarah	16

Savannah	44
Sawyer	48
Saylor	80
Scarlett	46
Schroeder	43
Scott	12
Sean	20
Sebastian	64
Selah	70
Selby	23
Selwyn	101
Sephora	39
Seraphina	59
Serena	98
Shavonne	15
Shayna	108
Shea	19
Sheldon	105
Sherry	17
Shiloh	56
Shirley	76
Shoshana	97
Sienna	46
Signe	101
Simona	65
Sinclair	83
Skipper	85
Skye	56
Slate	47
Sloane	102
Smith	81
Solana	110
Solveig	75

Sonder	71
Sonnet	113
Sonny	78
Sophie	22
Sophronia	95
Soren	94
Sparrow	84
Spencer	80
Sperry	71
Spike	54
Stanley	38
Stegg	55
Stein	63
Stephanie	14
Steven	10
Storri	28
Sullivan	24
Summer	72
Sumner	31
Sunday	112
Sunny	34
Sybella	25
Sybil	52
Sydney	44
Sylvan	106
Sylvie	100
Talia	110
Talmadge	9
Tam	21
Tamarind	61
Tana	15
Tanner	33
Tarik	65

Tate	100
Tatum	22
Taylor	80
Temperance	89
Tempest	111
Tennessee	51
Tennyson	25
Terra	62
Tessa	86
Thalassa	35
Thankful	89
Thatcher	81
Thelma	51
Theodore	30
Theseus	75
Thisbe	53
Thomas	8
Thora	111
Tide	85
Tiffany	12
Tilly	78
Timothy	12
Titan	54
Titania	57
Titus	104
Todd	42
Tolliver	87
Torrence	13
Townsend	95
Tracy	12
Tressa	13
Trevor	16
Trinity	97

Tripp	20
Tristan	68
Truly	88
Tyler	18
Tylus	29
Tyra	54
Ula	35
Uma	65
Valentino	68
Valeria	70
Valkyrie	73
Vance	77
Vanderbilt	83
Veda	87
Velda	9
Velma	91
Velvet	113
Venus	99
Vera	23
Verity	89
Vermilion	101
Vern	21
Vernon	31
Verona	45
Veronica	26
Vespera	77
Vicky	10
Vienna	45
Vincent	32
Vintage	28
Viola	66
Violet	30
Virginia	92

Viridian	47
Virtue	89
Viveca	25
Vivian	36
Vonda	13
Wainwright	81
Walker	80
Wally	78
Walter	94
Warner	43
Watson	23
Waylon	51
Webb	81
Wednesday	53
Wendell	17
Wesley	76
Westwood	106
Whitaker	59
Whitley	108
Wilbur	91
Wiley	86
Wilford	11
Willa	86
William	40
Willow	36
Wilson	38
Winifred	67
Winnie	79
Winston	90
Winter	58
Winthrop	83
Wisteria	53
Wolfgang	71

Wrangler	39
Wren	56
Wrestling	89
Wrinley	28
Wyatt	50
Wynn	21
Wystan	63
Wyvern	55
Xavier	73
Xeno	55
Xiomara	27
Yasmeen	19
Ynes	93
Yolanda	77
Yoli	107
Zachary	18
Zale	35
Zander	19
Zane	20
Zara	41
Zeal	113
Zee	29
Zelda	103
Zelma	9
Zenith	57
Zephyr	111
Ziggy	79
Zion	96
Ziva	65
Zoe	90
Zola	31
Zora	67
Zuriel	63

ACKNOWLEDGMENTS

Thank you to the women who helped me bring this project to life:

Book Cover Design: Madison Lee

Editor: Allison Buehner

Formatter: Catherine Downen

Copywriter: Sarah Taveras

Sleuth: Courtney Marti

Project Manager: Laura Briggs

Main Websites Used in Research:

Social Security Administration Baby Names

Behind the Name

Wiktionary

Nameberry

Thank you to Iain. None of this is possible without your love and support.

Thank you to my audience, my community; to everyone who follows Names With Steph.

You inspire me with your incredible suggestions, and you help me stay at the top of my game with your fantastic questions. Thank you for cheering me on and supporting me through the wins and the challenges. This all exists because of you and I will be forever grateful.

ABOUT THE AUTHOR

Steph Coffield is a professional name consultant, content creator, and the unofficial queen of all things whimsical. Her adoration of names came early, an interest first sparked while thoughtfully selecting the name Samantha for her Cabbage Patch Kid. While in the process of naming her own children, Steph's enthusiasm evolved into a deep love for the art of naming. She knew she wanted to share her passion with others. In 2021, she turned her passion into a profession. Since then, Steph has provided name consultation services to hundreds of clients, helping them choose the perfect moniker for their needs. She's also shared name inspiration with hundreds of thousands through her social media content, racking up over 15 million "likes."

When she's not curating name orders or creating social media content, she can be found sipping on an iced vanilla latte, binging the latest season of *Bridgerton*, or spending time with her family. A proud Midwesterner, Steph lives in Minnesota with her husband and three children. She is the author of two books, *Names Don't Have a Gender* and *Names Don't Have an Age*.

Connect with her on TikTok, Instagram, and YouTube @nameswithsteph or visit her website www.nameswithsteph.com

For exclusive content, join her at www.patreon.com/NamesWithSteph

To connect with Steph (or choose her to be your name consultant!), learn more at www.NamesWithSteph.com

www.ingramcontent.com/pod-product-compliance
Lightning Source LLC
Chambersburg PA
CBHW071324140726
47996CB00005B/1812

9 798218 427139